Demystifying Blockchain: A Practical Guide For Investors And Creatives

Hakop Simitian

PART 2: INTRODUCTION TO BLOCKCHAIN

Welcome to the world of blockchain! This revolutionary technology has the potential to transform the way investors and creatives produce, distribute, and monetize their work. In this ebook, we'll demystify blockchain and explore its practical applications for investors and creatives like you. We'll discuss how blockchain can help you protect your digital assets, connect with your audience, and build a more sustainable and equitable creative practice.

Blockchain technology, at its core, is a decentralized and transparent system for recording and verifying information. Imagine a digital ledger that's shared among a vast network of computers, where each transaction or piece of data is meticulously recorded and linked to the one before it. This creates an immutable and tamper-proof record of every activity, ensuring that the information remains secure and trustworthy.

For investors and creatives, this has profound implications. It offers a way to establish irrefutable proof of ownership for digital creations, preventing unauthorized reproduction or distribution. It also enables the creation of unique digital assets, like NFTs, that can be securely bought, sold, and traded, opening up new avenues for monetizing creative work.

Moreover, blockchain fosters trust and transparency between creators and their audiences. By providing a clear and auditable history of transactions, it builds confidence in the authenticity and provenance of creative works. This can lead to stronger relationships with fans and collectors, who can directly support investors through decentralized platforms and patronage systems.

In essence, blockchain empowers investors and creatives by giving them greater control over their work and its value. It provides the tools to protect intellectual property, connect with audiences in innovative ways, and participate in a more equitable and sustainable creative ecosystem. As you delve deeper into this ebook, you'll discover how blockchain can revolutionize your creative practice and unlock new possibilities for your artistic journey.

CHAPTER 1: WHAT IS BLOCKCHAIN?

Imagine a digital ledger, similar to a record book, but instead of being kept in a single location, it's shared publicly among countless computers across the globe. This ledger meticulously tracks every transaction, every piece of information exchanged, creating an unbroken chain of records. This, in essence, is a blockchain – a revolutionary technology that provides a secure, transparent, and tamper-proof way to store and verify data.

Now, let's break down what makes blockchain so special. Unlike traditional record-keeping systems that rely on a central authority like a bank or government to maintain the ledger, blockchain distributes it across a vast network of computers. This means that no single entity controls the information, making it incredibly difficult to manipulate or corrupt. Think of it as a shared responsibility, where everyone on the network has a copy of the ledger and participates in validating new entries.

Each new transaction or piece of data is bundled into a "block," which is then linked to the previous block using cryptography, forming a chronological "chain" of information. This chain is constantly growing as new blocks are added, creating a permanent and tamper-proof record of all activities.

One of the most remarkable features of blockchain is its immutability. Once a block is added to the chain, the information within it cannot be altered or deleted. This ensures the integrity and authenticity of the data, making it ideal for tracking ownership, verifying transactions, and establishing provenance. Imagine trying to erase something written in permanent ink on a piece of paper – it's nearly impossible. Similarly, altering information on a blockchain is extremely difficult, requiring immense computational power and the consensus of the majority of the network.

Furthermore, blockchain operates with unparalleled transparency. All transactions recorded on the blockchain are publicly viewable and traceable by anyone on the network. This openness fosters trust and accountability, as every action leaves an indelible mark. This is like having a public bulletin board where everyone can see the transactions, ensuring fairness and preventing any hidden dealings.

To ensure security, blockchain employs cryptography, the art of writing or solving codes. Cryptography safeguards data and prevents unauthorized access, making it extremely difficult to hack or manipulate the blockchain. Think of it as a complex lock that protects the information on the blockchain, making it secure from unauthorized access.

In essence, blockchain is a powerful tool for establishing trust, transparency, and security in a digital world. Its ability to create an immutable, verifiable, and shared record of information has far-reaching implications across various industries, and as we'll explore in the coming chapters, it holds immense potential for investors and creatives like you. It's like having a digital notary public that verifies and timestamps your creations, ensuring your rights and ownership are protected.

Are you ready to move on to the next chapter, where we'll explore why investors and creatives should care about blockchain?

CHAPTER 2: WHY SHOULD INVESTORS AND CREATIVES CARE ABOUT BLOCKCHAIN?

The digital age has revolutionized how investors and creatives produce, share, and engage with their work. Yet, it has also brought forth a unique set of challenges. Copyright infringement runs rampant online, with digital creations easily copied and distributed without permission. Artists often struggle to receive fair compensation for their work, with intermediaries taking significant cuts or platforms exploiting their content. Moreover, the lack of control over how their work is used and circulated can be frustrating and disheartening.

This is where blockchain comes in. This transformative technology offers solutions to many of these challenges, empowering investors and creatives to take back control of their digital creations and build a more sustainable and equitable creative practice.

One of the most significant benefits of blockchain for investors is its ability to protect their intellectual property. By recording the creation and ownership of digital assets on an immutable ledger, blockchain provides irrefutable proof of authenticity and provenance. This makes it much harder for others to steal or misuse your work without your permission. Imagine having a digital timestamp and certificate of authenticity for your creations, embedded in the very fabric of the internet.

Blockchain also enables investors to connect directly with their audience and monetize their work without relying on intermediaries. Through decentralized platforms and marketplaces, investors can sell their creations, offer exclusive content, and receive payments directly from their fans. This cuts out the middleman, ensuring that investors receive a larger share of the revenue generated from their work.

Furthermore, blockchain fosters transparency and trust between creators and their supporters. By providing a clear and auditable history of transactions, it builds confidence in the authenticity and value of creative works. This can lead to stronger relationships with fans and collectors, who can directly support investors through crowdfunding, patronage, or micropayments.

In essence, blockchain offers investors and creatives a new paradigm for managing and distributing their work. It provides the tools to protect their creations, get paid fairly, and connect with their audience in more meaningful ways. By understanding and embracing this technology, investors can navigate the challenges of the digital age and build a more sustainable and fulfilling creative career.

CHAPTER 3: HOW CAN BLOCKCHAIN BENEFIT INVESTORS AND CREATIVES?

Blockchain technology offers a wealth of opportunities for investors and creatives to revolutionize how they manage, distribute, and monetize their work. It's like a digital toolbox filled with innovative solutions to long-standing challenges in the creative industries. Let's explore how blockchain can empower you on your artistic journey.

Protecting Your Creative Work

One of the most significant benefits of blockchain for investors is its ability to protect intellectual property. In the digital realm, where copying and sharing are effortless, it's often difficult to prove ownership and prevent unauthorized use of creative works. Blockchain provides a solution by creating an immutable and transparent record of ownership.

Imagine registering your artwork, music, or writing on a blockchain. This creates a permanent and tamper-proof timestamp and certificate of authenticity, embedded in the very fabric of the internet. Should anyone attempt to steal or misuse your work, you have irrefutable proof of ownership to support your claim. This not only protects your rights but also deters potential infringers, fostering a more respectful and fair creative environment.

Monetizing Your Creations Directly

Traditionally, investors have relied on intermediaries such as galleries, record labels, or publishing houses to reach their audience and monetize their work. These intermediaries often take significant cuts, leaving investors with a smaller share of the revenue. Blockchain disrupts this model by enabling investors to connect directly with their fans and sell their creations without intermediaries.

Through decentralized platforms and marketplaces, investors can showcase their work, set their prices, and receive payments directly from their supporters. This eliminates the need for agents or distributors, allowing investors to retain a larger portion of their earnings. Moreover, blockchain facilitates micropayments and tipping, enabling fans to support their favorite investors with small amounts of cryptocurrency, fostering a more sustainable and direct patronage system.

Building Stronger Relationships with Your Audience

Blockchain not only facilitates monetization but also fosters deeper connections between investors and their audience. By creating transparent and auditable records of transactions, blockchain builds trust and confidence in the authenticity and value of creative works.

Imagine a collector purchasing an NFT of your artwork. They can trace the entire history of ownership on the blockchain, verifying its authenticity and provenance. This transparency increases the value of your work and strengthens the bond between you and your collector.

Furthermore, blockchain enables the creation of token-gated communities, where investors can offer exclusive content, rewards, and experiences to their most loyal fans. This fosters a sense of belonging and encourages deeper engagement with your audience.

Unlocking New Possibilities for Creative Expression

Beyond these practical benefits, blockchain also opens up new possibilities for creative expression and collaboration. The decentralized nature of blockchain encourages experimentation and innovation, allowing investors to explore new forms of art and storytelling.

For example, investors can create interactive artworks that evolve based on audience participation or collaborate on decentralized projects where ownership and contributions are transparently recorded on the blockchain. This fosters a more inclusive and collaborative creative environment, where investors can connect, share ideas, and co-create in innovative ways.

In conclusion, blockchain offers a wealth of benefits for investors and creatives. It's a powerful tool for protecting intellectual property, monetizing work directly, building stronger relationships with your audience, and unlocking new possibilities for creative expression. By embracing this technology, investors can navigate the challenges of the digital age and build a more sustainable, equitable, and fulfilling creative career.

PART 2 REVIEW: UNLOCKING THE BLOCKCHAIN

In Part 2 of this guide, we embarked on a journey to demystify blockchain technology. We started by exploring the fundamental question, "What is blockchain?" We likened it to a digital ledger, distributed across a vast network of computers, ensuring security, transparency, and immutability.

We then delved into why investors and creatives should care about this revolutionary technology. We discussed how blockchain offers solutions to challenges such as copyright infringement, unfair compensation, and lack of control over creative works.

Finally, we explored the multitude of ways blockchain can benefit investors and creatives. From protecting intellectual property and enabling direct monetization to fostering stronger relationships with fans and unlocking new avenues for creative expression, blockchain empowers investors to take control of their digital creations and build a more sustainable and fulfilling creative career.

Now, as we move into Part 3, we'll take a closer look at blockchain fundamentals. Get ready to discover how this technology is transforming the creative landscape and opening up exciting new possibilities for artistic expression, collaboration, and community building.

PART 3: BLOCKCHAIN FUNDAMENTALS

To truly harness the power of blockchain for your creative endeavors, it's essential to grasp its core principles. These fundamental concepts, (decentralization, immutability, transparency, and security)are the building blocks upon which blockchain's unique capabilities rest. They underpin its potential to revolutionize how investors and creatives manage, distribute, and even conceive of their work.

CHAPTER 4: DECENTRALIZATION: TAKING CONTROL OF YOUR CREATIVE DESTINY

Decentralization. It's a word that's often thrown around in the blockchain space, but what does it truly mean for you as an artist or creative? In essence, decentralization is about shifting power away from centralized authorities and distributing it amongst the many. It's about breaking free from the traditional gatekeepers and taking control of your own creative destiny.

Imagine a world where you no longer have to rely on galleries, record labels, or publishing houses to showcase and distribute your work. A world where you can connect directly with your audience, set your own prices, and retain full control over your creative output. This is the promise of decentralization, and it's one of the most powerful aspects of blockchain technology.

For centuries, investors and creatives have been at the mercy of intermediaries. These gatekeepers controlled access to audiences, dictated terms, and often took a significant cut of the profits. This centralized model often left investors feeling disempowered and undervalued.

Blockchain, with its decentralized nature, disrupts this traditional power dynamic. It allows investors to bypass intermediaries and connect directly with their fans, fostering a more equitable and transparent creative ecosystem. Think of it as cutting out the middleman and establishing a direct line of communication between you and your supporters.

This newfound freedom has profound implications for investors and creatives. You're no longer bound by the restrictive contracts and unfair revenue splits imposed by intermediaries. You have the autonomy to decide how your work is presented, priced, and distributed. Decentralized platforms and marketplaces provide access to a global audience, breaking down geographical barriers and connecting you with fans and collectors worldwide. By interacting directly with your audience, you can foster deeper connections and build a loyal community around your work. Without the constraints of traditional gatekeepers, you're free to explore new forms of creative expression and push the boundaries of your art.

Decentralization is not just about technology; it's about empowerment. It's about giving investors and creatives the tools they need to thrive in the digital age. By embracing decentralization, you can take control of your creative destiny and build a more sustainable and fulfilling artistic career.

CHAPTER 5: IMMUTABILITY: THE ENDURING POWER OF BLOCKCHAIN

Immutability. It's a cornerstone of blockchain technology, and for investors and creatives, it's a game-changer. In the simplest terms, immutability means that once data is recorded on a blockchain, it cannot be altered or tampered with. It's like etching your creation in stone, ensuring its integrity and authenticity for eternity.

Think of a traditional art gallery. A painting hangs on the wall, its history documented through certificates of authenticity and perhaps a record of previous owners. But what if someone were to forge those documents or even swap the painting for a clever fake? In the physical world, verifying authenticity can be a challenge. Now, imagine that same painting represented as a digital asset on a blockchain. The moment it's created, a record of its existence is permanently etched into the blockchain. Every detail, from the artist's name to the date of creation, is embedded within this immutable record. No one, not even the artist themselves, can alter this information.

This immutability has profound implications for investors and creatives. It provides unquestionable proof of ownership. Your creations are linked to you indelibly, protecting your rights and making it extremely difficult for someone to claim your work as their own. Collectors and fans can be confident in the genuineness of your work, knowing that its history and origin are verifiable and tamper-proof. The immutability of blockchain records adds a layer of trust and provenance to your creations, potentially increasing their value and desirability in the market.

Consider the challenges faced by musicians in the digital age. Their music can be easily copied and shared without permission, making it difficult to track ownership and ensure fair compensation. With blockchain, musicians can register their songs as unique digital assets, establishing a clear and permanent record of their rights. Or think of a writer who self-publishes their work online. Blockchain can provide a timestamped record of their authorship, protecting their intellectual property and preventing plagiarism.

Immutability is not just about security; it's about preserving the integrity of your creative work. It's about ensuring that your creations are recognized, valued, and protected in a digital world where copying and sharing are rampant. By understanding and utilizing the power of immutability, investors and creatives can safeguard their legacy and build a more sustainable future for their work.

CHAPTER 6: TRANSPARENCY: ILLUMINATING THE CREATIVE PROCESS

Transparency. It's a quality often praised but rarely fully achieved, especially in the often opaque world of art and commerce. Yet, blockchain brings a new level of openness to the creative process, where every transaction, every exchange, is recorded in a publicly viewable and traceable manner. This radical transparency increases accountability and trust within the system, benefiting both creators and their audiences.

Imagine a world where the journey of a piece of art, from its initial creation to its final owner, is laid bare for all to see. With blockchain, this is a reality. Each transaction involving a digital asset is recorded on the blockchain, creating an immutable and auditable history. This means that collectors can trace the provenance of a digital artwork, verifying its authenticity and ownership history with complete confidence.

This transparency fosters a sense of trust and accountability that is often lacking in traditional art markets. Artists can demonstrate the originality of their work and prove their ownership rights, while collectors can be assured of the value and legitimacy of their acquisitions. This openness can lead to fairer pricing, reduced fraud, and a more equitable distribution of revenue within the creative ecosystem.

Moreover, transparency can help build stronger relationships between investors and their fans. By openly sharing information about their creative process, investors can invite their audience to participate in their journey. This can foster a sense of community and shared ownership, strengthening the bond between creators and their supporters.

Think of a musician releasing a new album on a blockchain-based platform. Fans can not only purchase the album directly but also see how the revenue is distributed among the investors, producers, and collaborators. This transparency builds trust and allows fans to feel more connected to the music they love.

Or consider a writer who uses blockchain to publish their work. Readers can see the entire history of revisions and edits, gaining a deeper appreciation for the creative process. This transparency can also help combat plagiarism and ensure that writers receive proper credit for their work.

Transparency is not just about openness; it's about building trust, accountability, and stronger relationships within the creative community. By embracing the transparency offered by blockchain, investors and creatives can foster a more equitable and sustainable environment for their work to thrive.

CHAPTER 7: SECURITY: BUILDING FORTRESSES OF TRUST WITH CRYPTOGRAPHY

Security. In the vast, interconnected world of the internet, it's a paramount concern, especially when it comes to valuable digital assets. Blockchain, at its core, is built upon a foundation of security, employing the power of cryptography to safeguard data and prevent unauthorized access. This makes it incredibly difficult to hack or manipulate, providing a safe haven for investors and creatives to protect their work.

Imagine a digital vault, fortified with intricate locks and impenetrable walls. This is the level of security that cryptography brings to blockchain. Cryptography, the art and science of secret communication, uses complex algorithms to encrypt data, making it unreadable to anyone without the proper decryption key.

On the blockchain, cryptography is used to secure every transaction and piece of data. Each block is linked to the previous one using a unique cryptographic signature, creating an unbroken chain of trust. This ensures that any attempt to tamper with the data would be immediately detected, as it would disrupt the integrity of the entire chain.

Think of it as a digital fingerprint for every transaction. Any alteration, no matter how small, would change the fingerprint, alerting the network to the attempted fraud. This makes blockchain incredibly resistant to hacking and manipulation, providing a secure platform for investors and creatives to store and manage their digital assets.

This robust security has significant implications for the creative industries. Artists can rest assured that their creations are protected from theft and unauthorized distribution. Collectors can confidently invest in digital art, knowing that its authenticity and provenance are guaranteed by the blockchain's security measures.

Consider the world of online music distribution. Illegal downloads and unauthorized sharing have plagued the industry for years. With blockchain, musicians can distribute their music securely, preventing piracy and ensuring they receive fair compensation for their work.

Or imagine a photographer who wants to sell their images online. Blockchain provides a secure platform to showcase and sell their work, protecting their copyright and preventing unauthorized use.

Security is not just about preventing theft; it's about building trust. By providing a secure and reliable platform for creative works, blockchain fosters confidence and encourages innovation. Artists can focus on what they do best – creating – knowing that their work is protected by the powerful force of cryptography.

PART 3 REVIEW: THE PILLARS OF BLOCKCHAIN

In Part 3, we delved deeper into the core principles of blockchain, those foundational pillars that underpin its transformative power for investors and creatives. We explored decentralization, where power shifts from central authorities to the broader community, liberating investors from the constraints of traditional intermediaries.

We then examined immutability, the concept of an unalterable record, ensuring the integrity and authenticity of creative works for eternity. This permanence protects ownership, guarantees authenticity, and enhances the value of digital creations.

Next, we explored transparency, where every transaction is recorded openly and traceably on the blockchain. This fosters trust and accountability, enabling stronger relationships between investors and their audience while promoting fairness and ethical practices within the creative ecosystem.

Finally, we discussed security, fortified by the power of cryptography. Blockchain's robust security measures safeguard digital assets from unauthorized access and manipulation, providing a safe haven for investors to showcase and monetize their work.

With a firm grasp of these fundamental principles, you're well-prepared to embark on the next stage of our journey. In Part

4, we'll explore the exciting world of blockchain use cases for investors and creatives. Get ready to discover how this technology is revolutionizing the creative landscape and opening up new avenues for artistic expression, collaboration, and community building.

PART 4: BLOCKCHAIN IN ACTION - USE CASES FOR INVESTORS AND CREATIVES

Prepare to be amazed! We're about to step into a world where creativity and technology intertwine in unprecedented ways. Blockchain, with its secure and transparent nature, is revolutionizing how investors and creatives protect, share, and even monetize their work.

In this section, we'll explore real-world applications that are reshaping the creative landscape. From establishing undeniable ownership of digital artwork to forging deeper connections with fans and communities, blockchain offers a wealth of opportunities. Get ready to discover how this technology is empowering investors like never before, opening up exciting new avenues for creative expression and collaboration.

CHAPTER 8: DIGITAL ASSET OWNERSHIP AND MANAGEMENT

In the digital age, where creativity flourishes in the boundless realm of the internet, establishing ownership and managing digital assets has become paramount. Blockchain technology emerges as a powerful ally for investors and creatives, offering innovative solutions to protect their creations and navigate the complexities of the digital world.

One of the most groundbreaking applications of blockchain in the creative industries is the rise of Non-Fungible Tokens (NFTs). These unique digital tokens represent ownership of a specific digital or physical asset, such as a piece of artwork, a song, or even a virtual collectible. NFTs provide a way to verify authenticity and scarcity, enabling investors to sell and trade their work in new and exciting ways.

Imagine an artist creating a digital painting. By minting this artwork as an NFT, they establish an immutable record of ownership on the blockchain. This token serves as a digital certificate of authenticity, proving the artwork's origin and preventing unauthorized reproduction or distribution. Collectors can confidently purchase NFTs, knowing that they possess a unique and verifiable piece of digital art.

Furthermore, blockchain technology can revolutionize Digital Rights Management (DRM) systems. Traditional DRM systems have often been criticized for their restrictiveness and lack of transparency. Blockchain offers a more efficient and transparent approach, giving creators greater control over their intellectual property and how it is used and distributed.

Imagine a musician releasing a new song on a blockchain-based platform. They can embed specific usage rights within the NFT associated with the song, allowing fans to purchase the right to listen, share, or even remix the track. This gives investors granular control over their work while ensuring they receive fair compensation for its use.

Another crucial aspect of digital asset ownership is provenance tracking. Blockchain provides an immutable record of an artwork's history, tracing its ownership and creation journey. This provenance information is invaluable for collectors, as it adds a layer of trust and authenticity to the artwork, potentially increasing its value.

Imagine a collector acquiring a digital artwork through an NFT. They can trace the entire history of ownership on the blockchain, verifying its authenticity and tracing its journey from the artist's studio to their collection. This transparency not only builds confidence but also adds to the story and significance of the artwork.

In conclusion, blockchain technology offers a robust framework for digital asset ownership and management. Through NFTs, transparent DRM systems, and provenance tracking, investors and creatives can protect their work, control its distribution, and establish verifiable ownership in the digital realm.

CHAPTER 9: CONTENT MONETIZATION

In the digital age, monetizing creative work can be a complex endeavor. Artists and creatives often face challenges in getting fairly compensated for their efforts. Blockchain technology offers innovative solutions to these challenges, opening up new avenues for content monetization and empowering creators to take control of their financial destiny.

One of the most promising applications of blockchain in content monetization is the emergence of decentralized content platforms. These platforms allow creators to connect directly with their audience and monetize their work without relying on intermediaries such as publishers, record labels, or distributors. By cutting out the middleman, investors can retain a larger share of the revenue generated from their work and have greater control over how it is accessed and distributed.

Imagine a musician releasing a new album on a blockchain-based platform. They can set their own price for the album, offer exclusive content to their fans, and receive payments directly from listeners without a record label taking a significant cut. This direct-to-fan model empowers musicians and allows them to build stronger relationships with their supporters.

Another innovative approach to content monetization is tokenized licensing. Creators can use blockchain to tokenize licenses for their work, making it easier to track usage, automate royalty payments, and prevent unauthorized use. This provides a more efficient and transparent way to manage intellectual property rights and ensure that creators are fairly compensated for their work.

Imagine a photographer licensing their images for use in a magazine. By tokenizing the license on a blockchain, they can track where and how the image is used, automatically receive royalty payments each time it's published, and prevent unauthorized use or distribution. This gives photographers greater control over their work and ensures they receive fair compensation for its use.

Furthermore, blockchain enables micropayments and tipping, allowing fans to directly support their favorite investors and creators with small amounts of cryptocurrency. This opens up new possibilities for monetizing content that may not have been financially viable through traditional channels.

Imagine a writer publishing their work online. Readers can show their appreciation by sending micropayments or tips directly to the writer's digital wallet. This allows fans to support their favorite creators in a more direct and meaningful way, fostering a closer connection between investors and their audience.

Ultimately, blockchain hands the reins back to investors and creatives when it comes to monetizing their work. Through decentralized platforms, tokenized licensing, and micropayments, blockchain provides the tools and autonomy to shape their financial future and contribute to a more sustainable and equitable creative landscape.

CHAPTER 10: COMMUNITY BUILDING AND ENGAGEMENT

In the interconnected world of art and creativity, community plays a vital role. It's where investors connect with their audience, share ideas, and find support for their creative endeavors. Blockchain technology offers innovative ways to foster community building and engagement, empowering investors and creatives to cultivate deeper relationships with their fans and build thriving creative ecosystems.

One of the most exciting developments in this space is the rise of Decentralized Autonomous Organizations (DAOs). These community-led organizations are governed by rules encoded on a blockchain, providing a transparent and democratic way for investors and creatives to collaborate, share resources, and govern their communities.

Imagine a collective of investors forming a DAO to showcase their work, pool resources for exhibitions, and make decisions collectively through voting mechanisms on the blockchain. This fosters a sense of shared ownership and empowers investors to support each other while maintaining transparency and fairness within the community.

Another powerful tool for community building is the use of

token-gated communities. Creators can use tokens to create exclusive communities for their most loyal fans, offering special access, rewards, and experiences. This fosters a sense of belonging and encourages deeper engagement with the artist's work and creative process.

Imagine a musician creating a token-gated community for their most dedicated fans. Members could gain access to exclusive content, behind-the-scenes updates, and even participate in online listening parties or meet-and-greets. This creates a closer connection between the artist and their fans, fostering a sense of loyalty and shared passion for the music.

Furthermore, blockchain can facilitate crowdfunding and patronage, allowing fans to directly support the creation of new work and share in its success. This opens up new possibilities for investors to fund their projects and build a more sustainable creative practice.

Imagine an artist launching a crowdfunding campaign on a blockchain platform. Fans can contribute cryptocurrency to support the project and receive tokens that represent a share of the artwork's future value or grant access to exclusive rewards and experiences. This allows fans to become active participants in the creative process and share in the success of the artwork.

In conclusion, blockchain technology offers a range of powerful tools for community building and engagement. By enabling DAOs, token-gated communities, and crowdfunding initiatives, blockchain empowers investors and creatives to cultivate deeper relationships with their fans, build thriving creative ecosystems, and foster a more collaborative and supportive environment for artistic expression.

PART 4 REVIEW: BLOCKCHAIN IN THE CREATIVE WORLD

In Part 4, we explored the exciting ways blockchain is being used by investors and creatives. We started with **Digital Asset Ownership and Management**, where we learned how NFTs are revolutionizing the art world by providing a way to verify ownership and authenticity of digital creations. We also saw how blockchain can improve Digital Rights Management, giving creators more control over their work, and how it can be used to track the history of an artwork, adding to its value and trustworthiness.

Next, we delved into **Content Monetization**, where we discovered how blockchain empowers investors to connect directly with their audience and get paid fairly. We explored decentralized content platforms that cut out the middleman, tokenized licensing that automates royalty payments, and micropayments that allow fans to support creators directly.

Finally, we looked at **Community Building and Engagement**, where we learned how blockchain can help investors foster thriving communities around their work. We explored DAOs, which allow for collaborative decision-making, token-gated communities that offer exclusive access to loyal fans, and crowdfunding initiatives that enable fans to directly support the creation of new work.

Now, with a solid understanding of how blockchain is being used in the creative world, it's time to get hands-on. In Part 5, we'll provide a step-by-step guide to using blockchain, equipping you with the knowledge and tools to start your own blockchain journey.

PART 5: A STEP-BY-STEP GUIDE TO USING BLOCKCHAIN

Congratulations! You've made it this far, and you're now well-versed in the fundamentals of blockchain and its potential to revolutionize the creative landscape. You understand its core principles and how they can empower investors and creatives to protect their work, connect with their audience, and build a more sustainable and equitable creative practice. Now, it's time to put this knowledge into action.

This section provides a practical, step-by-step guide to help you get started with the essential tools and processes involved in using blockchain. We'll walk you through setting up a digital wallet, creating and minting NFTs, joining a DAO, and protecting your digital assets. Think of this as your blockchain toolkit, equipping you with the necessary skills and knowledge to navigate this exciting new world.

Whether you're an artist looking to tokenize your work, a musician seeking new ways to distribute your music, or a writer exploring innovative publishing models, this guide will provide you with the foundation to embark on your blockchain journey. So, let's dive in and start exploring the practical steps involved in harnessing the power of blockchain for your creative endeavors.

CHAPTER 11: SETTING UP A DIGITAL WALLET - YOUR GATEWAY TO THE BLOCKCHAIN WORLD

Think of a digital wallet as your passport to the world of blockchain. It's an essential tool for storing, managing, and accessing your cryptocurrencies and NFTs, just as a physical wallet holds your cash and cards. A digital wallet safeguards your digital assets and allows you to participate in the blockchain ecosystem, but it's important to remember that not all digital wallets are created equal. There are various types, each with its own features and security measures.

Hot wallets are connected to the internet, offering convenience and ease of use for frequent transactions. They're often browser extensions or mobile apps, allowing you to quickly access and manage your assets. MetaMask, Coinbase Wallet, and Trust Wallet are popular examples of hot wallets. For those prioritizing maximum security, cold wallets are the better option. These wallets store your assets offline, typically on a hardware device like a USB drive. This isolation from the internet makes them highly resistant to hacking and theft. Ledger and Trezor are well-known providers of cold wallets.

Custodial wallets are managed by a third party, such as a cryptocurrency exchange. While convenient for beginners, they entrust your assets to the custody of the provider. With non-custodial wallets, you have complete control over your assets and private keys. This offers greater security and autonomy but also places the responsibility of safeguarding your keys solely on you.

Choosing the right digital wallet depends on your individual needs and priorities. Consider factors such as security, ease of use, and compatibility with the blockchain platforms you intend to use. Once you've chosen a wallet, setting it up securely is paramount. This involves creating a strong, unique password and securely storing your seed phrase, a unique combination of words that grants access to your wallet. Treat your seed phrase like a precious treasure, keeping it offline and in a safe place, perhaps even consider multiple secure backups. Remember, losing your seed phrase means losing access to your digital assets, so safeguard it with utmost care.

With your digital wallet set up, you're ready to explore the vast possibilities of blockchain. You can now receive, store, and send cryptocurrencies, purchase NFTs, and participate in decentralized applications (dApps). Your wallet is your gateway to this exciting new world, empowering you to engage with the blockchain ecosystem and unlock its full potential.

CHAPTER 12: CREATING AND MINTING NFTS

NFTs, or non-fungible tokens, have revolutionized the art world by providing a way to represent ownership of digital assets on the blockchain. For investors and creatives, minting NFTs can open up new avenues for monetizing their work and connecting with their audience. But how do you actually create and mint your own NFT? Let's break down the process.

First, you'll need to choose a blockchain platform to mint your NFT on. Ethereum is the most popular choice for NFTs, but other platforms like Tezos, Solana, and Polygon are also gaining traction. Each platform has its own unique features, fees, and communities, so do your research to find the one that best suits your needs.

Next, you'll need to create your digital asset. This could be anything from a digital painting or photograph to a music track or video clip. Ensure that your artwork is in a format compatible with the blockchain platform you've chosen.

Once you have your digital asset ready, it's time to mint it as an NFT. This involves creating a unique token that represents your artwork on the blockchain. You'll need to use a digital wallet that supports NFT minting and pay a fee in cryptocurrency to cover the cost of the transaction.

Several platforms and marketplaces make minting NFTs easy

and accessible. Popular options include OpenSea, Rarible, and SuperRare. These platforms provide user-friendly interfaces and tools to guide you through the minting process.

When minting your NFT, you'll have the option to add various attributes and metadata, such as the artwork's title, description, and even unlockable content for collectors. This information helps to enhance the value and uniqueness of your NFT.

Once your NFT is minted, it's ready to be shared with the world. You can list it for sale on NFT marketplaces, showcase it on your website or social media channels, and even use it to access exclusive communities or events.

Minting NFTs can be a powerful way for investors and creatives to monetize their work, connect with their audience, and participate in the growing world of digital art and collectibles.

CHAPTER 13: JOINING A DAO

DAOs, or Decentralized Autonomous Organizations, are a revolutionary concept in community governance and collaboration. Imagine a group of like-minded individuals coming together with shared goals, their collective decisions and actions transparently recorded and automatically executed on the blockchain. This, in essence, is the power of a DAO.

For investors and creatives, DAOs offer a new paradigm for collaboration, resource sharing, and community governance. They provide a platform to connect with fellow investors, collectors, and enthusiasts, fostering a sense of shared ownership and collective decision-making.

Joining a DAO is like becoming a member of a self-governing collective. You typically acquire tokens that represent your membership and voting rights within the organization. These tokens can be earned through contributions to the DAO or purchased on cryptocurrency exchanges.

Once you're a member, you can participate in the governance of the DAO by proposing and voting on proposals that shape the organization's direction. This could include decisions about funding projects, allocating resources, or setting community guidelines.

DAOs offer various benefits for investors and creatives. They can provide access to funding opportunities, collaborative projects, and shared resources such as studio spaces or exhibition opportunities. They also foster a sense of community and belonging, connecting investors with like-minded individuals and creating a supportive environment for creative exploration.

Furthermore, DAOs can help investors and creatives navigate the complexities of the digital age. By pooling resources and knowledge, DAOs can provide support in areas such as legal and financial advice, marketing and promotion, and even mental health and well-being.

Joining a DAO is an exciting opportunity to become part of a self-governing community and participate in shaping the future of creative collaboration. It's a chance to connect with fellow investors, share resources, and contribute to a more equitable and sustainable creative ecosystem.

CHAPTER 14: PROTECTING YOUR DIGITAL ASSETS

Navigating the blockchain world opens up exciting opportunities, but it's essential to be aware of the security risks and take proactive steps to protect your valuable digital assets. Think of it as safeguarding your treasure chest in a digital landscape.

First and foremost, **secure your digital wallet**. Choose a reputable wallet provider and create a strong, unique password. Never share your password or seed phrase with anyone, and store them securely offline. Consider using a password manager to generate and store your passwords safely.

Be wary of **phishing scams and fraudulent websites**. Always double-check the URL and security certificate of any website you interact with, especially when entering your wallet credentials or making transactions. Avoid clicking on suspicious links or downloading attachments from unknown sources.

Keep your **software and devices updated**. Regularly update your operating system, web browser, and digital wallet to benefit from the latest security patches and bug fixes. This helps protect you from vulnerabilities that could be exploited by malicious actors.

When interacting with dApps or smart contracts, exercise caution and **do your research**. Only interact with reputable platforms and carefully review the terms and conditions before connecting your wallet or making transactions. Be mindful of potential risks such as scams or vulnerabilities in the code.

Consider using a **hardware wallet** for added security. These devices store your private keys offline, providing an extra layer of protection against hacking and theft.

Remember, **you are responsible for the security of your digital assets**. While blockchain technology offers robust security measures, it's crucial to take precautions and stay informed about potential risks. By practicing good security hygiene and staying vigilant, you can safeguard your digital treasures and navigate the blockchain world with confidence.

PART 5 REVIEW: YOUR BLOCKCHAIN TOOLKIT

In Part 5, we shifted from theory to practice, equipping you with the essential tools and knowledge to embark on your blockchain journey. We started with setting up a digital wallet, your gateway to the blockchain world. We explored different types of wallets, from hot wallets for frequent transactions to cold wallets for maximum security, emphasizing the importance of choosing the right wallet and securing your seed phrase.

Next, we delved into the exciting world of NFTs, learning how to create and mint these unique digital assets that represent ownership of your creative work on the blockchain. We explored various platforms and marketplaces for minting NFTs and discussed the importance of adding metadata to enhance their value and uniqueness.

We then ventured into the realm of DAOs, or Decentralized Autonomous Organizations, discovering how to join these self-governing communities and participate in their governance and activities. We highlighted the benefits of DAOs for investors and creatives, including access to funding, collaborative projects, and shared resources.

Finally, we emphasized the importance of protecting your digital assets in the blockchain landscape. We discussed security best practices, such as securing your digital wallet, being wary of phishing scams, keeping your software updated, and exercising caution when interacting with dApps and smart contracts.

With a solid understanding of these practical steps, you're well-prepared to navigate the blockchain world and harness its potential for your creative endeavors. Now, as we move into Part 6, we'll explore the future of blockchain and its implications for the creative industries. Get ready to envision the possibilities and challenges that lie ahead as this transformative technology continues to evolve.

PART 6: GAZING INTO THE CRYSTAL BALL - THE FUTURE OF BLOCKCHAIN

We've journeyed through the fundamentals of blockchain, explored its core principles, and delved into its practical applications for investors and creatives. Now, let's turn our gaze towards the horizon and contemplate the future of this transformative technology.

The use of blockchain in the creative industries is still in its early stages, but it's evolving at an electrifying pace. New possibilities and applications are emerging constantly, pushing the boundaries of what's possible and reshaping the creative landscape in profound ways.

In this section, we'll explore the trends and innovations that are shaping the future of blockchain for investors and creatives. We'll delve into the potential impact of this technology on the creative industries, examining both the challenges and opportunities that lie ahead.

Get ready to envision a future where investors and creatives have greater control over their work, connect with their audience in more meaningful ways, and participate in a more equitable and sustainable creative ecosystem. The future of blockchain is brimming with potential, and this section will serve as your guide to navigating this exciting and ever-evolving landscape.

CHAPTER 15: EMERGING TRENDS AND TECHNOLOGIES

The blockchain space is a hotbed of innovation, with new trends and technologies constantly emerging. As an artist or creative, staying ahead of the curve can unlock exciting new possibilities for your work and career. Let's explore some of the most promising trends on the horizon.

The Metaverse

The metaverse is a collective term for immersive digital worlds where users can interact with each other, participate in experiences, and even create and trade digital assets. Blockchain technology plays a crucial role in the metaverse by enabling the ownership and transfer of virtual land, digital art, and other virtual goods. For investors and creatives, the metaverse offers new avenues for creative expression, collaboration, and community building. Imagine creating and showcasing your artwork in a virtual gallery, collaborating with other investors on immersive installations, or even designing and selling virtual fashion or accessories.

Web3

Web3 is the vision for a decentralized internet built on blockchain technology. It aims to shift power away from centralized platforms and give users greater control over their data and online identity. For investors and creatives, Web3 offers the potential to connect directly with their audience, monetize their work without intermediaries, and participate in a more equitable and transparent online ecosystem. Imagine publishing your writing on a decentralized platform where you retain full ownership and control over your content or releasing your music directly to fans without relying on a record label.

Decentralized Social Media

Decentralized social media platforms are emerging as an alternative to traditional social media giants. These platforms are built on blockchain technology, giving users greater control over their data and privacy. For investors and creatives, decentralized social media offers a way to connect with their audience in a more authentic and meaningful way, free from censorship and algorithmic manipulation. Imagine sharing your work on a platform where your content reaches your followers directly, without being filtered or restricted by algorithms.

These emerging trends and technologies hold immense potential for investors and creatives. By staying informed and embracing innovation, you can position yourself at the forefront of the creative revolution powered by blockchain.

CHAPTER 16: THE BLOCKCHAIN HORIZON: NAVIGATING THE FUTURE OF CREATIVITY

The blockchain revolution is still unfolding, and its full impact on the creative industries is yet to be realized. As investors and creatives, it's essential to not only understand the current applications but also to look ahead, anticipate the challenges, and embrace the opportunities that this evolving technology presents.

Blockchain has the potential to disrupt traditional models of content creation, distribution, and monetization. Imagine a world where investors connect directly with their audience, bypassing intermediaries like record labels, publishers, and galleries. Decentralized platforms could empower creators to set their own terms, receive fairer compensation, and maintain greater control over their work.

This shift towards a more equitable and sustainable creative ecosystem could foster greater artistic freedom and diversity. Artists from marginalized communities could gain access to global markets and funding opportunities, breaking down barriers and fostering a more inclusive creative landscape.

However, this journey towards a blockchain-powered future is not without its challenges. Scalability, environmental concerns, and regulatory uncertainty are some of the hurdles that need to be addressed.

Scalability refers to the ability of blockchain networks to handle a growing number of transactions. As adoption increases, ensuring that these networks can handle the volume and complexity of transactions efficiently is crucial.

The environmental impact of blockchain technology, particularly those that rely on energy-intensive consensus mechanisms like Proof-of-Work, is another concern. The creative community needs to advocate for and adopt more sustainable blockchain solutions.

Furthermore, the regulatory landscape surrounding blockchain is still evolving. Clear and supportive regulations are essential to foster innovation and protect investors and consumers alike.

Navigating this evolving landscape requires adaptability, awareness, and a willingness to experiment. Artists and creatives who embrace the opportunities and address the challenges head-on will be well-positioned to thrive in the blockchain-powered future.

By staying informed, engaging with the community, and actively participating in shaping the future of blockchain, investors can harness its transformative power to build a more equitable, sustainable, and creatively fulfilling world.

PART 6 REVIEW: SHAPING THE FUTURE OF CREATIVITY

In Part 6, we gazed into the crystal ball and explored the exciting future possibilities of blockchain for investors and creatives. We began with Chapter 15, "Emerging Trends and Technologies," where we discussed the rise of the metaverse, Web3, and decentralized social media. These innovations offer new avenues for creative expression, collaboration, and community building, empowering investors to connect with their audience in more meaningful ways and participate in a more equitable and transparent online ecosystem.

In Chapter 16, "The Blockchain Horizon: Navigating the Future of Creativity," we explored the potential impact of blockchain on the creative industries. We discussed how blockchain could disrupt traditional models of content creation, distribution, and monetization, leading to a more equitable and sustainable creative ecosystem. We also examined the challenges and opportunities that blockchain presents for investors and creatives, emphasizing the importance of adaptability, awareness, and active participation in shaping the future of this transformative technology.

PART 1: YOUR BLOCKCHAIN WANDERLUST BEGINS.

This isn't truly an ending, but rather a commencement. You've reached the final pages of this guide, but it's merely the first step on your journey into the boundless realm of blockchain. Look how far you've come! From grasping the fundamental essence of blockchain to envisioning its potential to reshape the creative landscape, you now possess the knowledge and tools to navigate this transformative technology with unwavering confidence.

Recall the spark of possibility when you first held a paintbrush, a musical instrument, or a pen. It was a moment of discovery, of endless potential. Blockchain offers that same sense of wonder and opportunity for investors and creatives. It's a blank canvas, a new stage, a fresh page waiting to be filled with your unique creative vision.

Throughout this book, we've demystified blockchain, peeling back its layers to reveal the core principles that drive its power. We've explored decentralization, immutability, transparency, and security, highlighting how these concepts can empower you to protect your creative work, forge deeper connections with your audience, and build a more sustainable and equitable creative practice.

We've ventured into the exciting world of NFTs, those unique digital tokens that represent ownership of your creations on the blockchain. We've delved into the realm of DAOs, those self-governing communities where collaboration and collective decision-making thrive. And we've equipped you with the practical knowledge to set up a digital wallet, mint your own NFTs, and safeguard your digital assets.

Now, it's time to seize the reins and embark on your own blockchain odyssey. Embrace the boundless opportunities that this technology presents. Experiment, innovate, and connect with the vibrant community of blockchain enthusiasts and creators.

Remember, blockchain is more than just lines of code and complex algorithms; it's a movement. It's about empowering investors and creatives like you to take control of your work, your careers, and your financial future. It's about building a more equitable and sustainable creative ecosystem where every artist has the opportunity to thrive.

So, go forth and create. Explore the uncharted territories of this new frontier. Build your financial fortress with the bricks of knowledge you've gained. The blockchain revolution is here, and you're not just a witness, but an active participant. Your blockchain wanderlust begins now.